ASSEMBLY LINES

Jane Commane was born in Coventry and lives and works in Warwickshire. Her first full-length collection, *Assembly Lines*, was published by Bloodaxe in 2018. She has been a poet in residence at the Brontë Parsonage in Haworth, and has led many writing workshops in a variety of locations, including in museums, castles, city centres, orchards and along riverbanks. In 2016, she was chosen to join Writing West Midlands' Room 204 writer development programme. A graduate of the Warwick Writing Programme, for a decade she also worked in museums and archives.

She is editor at Nine Arches Press, co-editor of *Under the Radar* magazine, co-organiser of the Leicester Shindig poetry series, and is co-author (with Jo Bell) of *How to Be a Poet*, a creative writing handbook and blog series. In 2017 she was awarded a Jerwood Compton Poetry Fellowship.

JANE COMMANE

Assembly Lines

BLOODAXE BOOKS

ISBN: 978 1 78037 408 6

First published 2018 by
Bloodaxe Books Ltd,
Eastburn,
South Park,
Hexham,
Northumberland NE46 1BS.

www.bloodaxebooks.com
For further information about Bloodaxe titles
please visit our website or write to
the above address for a catalogue.

Supported using public funding by

**ARTS COUNCIL
ENGLAND**

Cover design: Neil Astley & Pamela Robertson-Pearce.

Printed in Great Britain by Bell & Bain Limited, Glasgow, Scotland, on
acid-free paper sourced from mills with FSC chain of custody certification.

for Mum & Dad

ACKNOWLEDGEMENTS

I am grateful to the following magazines and journals where some of these poems have previously appeared: *And Other Poems, Anon, Bare fiction, Gists & Piths, Hand + Star, Iota, Litter, The Morning Star, The North, Proletarian Poetry, The Stare's Nest, Tears in the Fence* and *The Warwick Review.*

Some of these poems have also featured in anthologies, including *The Voyage* (University of Warwick / Monash University), ed. Chandani Lokuge & David Morley (Silkworms Ink, 2011), *Lung Jazz: Young British Poets for Oxfam*, ed. Todd Swift, Kim Lockwood (Cinnamon Press, 2011), and The Best British Poetry 2011, ed. Roddy Lumsden (Salt Publishing, 2011).

The epigraph quoting a Joel Lane poem is from 'Echoland' from *Trouble in the Heartland* (Arc Publications, 2004). The epigraph quoting a Manic Street Preachers' song is from 'Design for Life'. The poem 'National Curriculum' makes reference to song titles and lyrics by The Smiths, The Jesus and Mary Chain and Manic Street Preachers.

'Odds On': The Irish racehorse Arkle was reputedly so famous that he was referred to as 'Himself' and would receive fan mail addressed 'Himself, Ireland'. Legend has it his performance was down to a twice-daily Guinness habit. His skeleton can be seen in the museum of the Irish National Stud. After the economic crisis of 2008 in Ireland, which followed the 'Celtic Tiger' boom years, there was a large increase in horses (and especially racehorses) sent to abattoirs (see reference: http://www.bbc.co.uk/news/world-europe-12682680)

'Seven Horse Secrets' was recorded and featured as part of the University of Warwick's 50th Anniversary celebrations: http://www2.warwick.ac.uk/about/warwick50/blog/50thpoetry/seven-horse-secrets

'On Discovery' was featured in the anthology *MAP: Poems after William Smith and his 1815 Geological Map* (Worple Press, 2015).

'Dresden Papers' was featured in *Iris of the Peeping Eye* (Five Seasons / Birmingham Museums and Art Gallery, 2013) and responds to 'Dresden, 1945', an artwork by Matthew Picton, in the collection of the Herbert Art Gallery and Museum, Coventry.

The poem 'Landmarks' was written for and featured on the 'Against Rape' series of poems on the *Peony Moon* blog.

CONTENTS

9   Here, once
10 National Curriculum
15 Sand
16 On the New Bypass
17 Fabrikgeist
18 The Shop-floor Gospel
20 Coventry is
22 Midlands kids,
23 Our Old Lady of the Rain
24 Love Song for the Ordnance Survey
26 Border Dispute
27 On Discovery
29 Odds On
30 Seven Horse Secrets
31 Dog, on First Being Named
32 The hearts of everyone in this room
33 Script Notes from the lost episode of *The Future*
34 UnWeather
37 Reasoning
38 Three Sketches for Dreams
41 Double Exposure
42 Gasbagging
43 Folklore
44 Shrug
45 How we fell in love with big data
46 How the Town Lost Its Song
49 The poem written to settle an old score is
50 Lonely Hearts
51 Landmarks
52 Disturbed
53 Dresden Papers
55 The Ghost Light
56 Otters, Avon
57 Shrapnel
59 Around the Rectory
60 Circa
61 Homing
62 Poem in which a small dog looks into the sun

If you can touch this landscape,
be part of it, you'll never leave.

JOEL LANE

To wear the scars, to show from where I came.

MANIC STREET PREACHERS

Here, once

Chasing the odours of burnt pocketbooks,
to teenage angst plotted roughly some time
between *glasnost* and *things can only get better*,

led by the nose to the horse pool, no idea of escape,
the shakings and trembling in the hedges
of something-something summers to come.

In a reel of suburban dogs barking, gulls rising a *V* across
the sunset in the near that bleeds umber and gold
onto four walls once long with Thatcherite shadows,

and in the knowing that one day it would all be
in the middle distance, a seam of light is struck
to fade the poster of a one-hit wonder.

National Curriculum

I *History*

At the revisionist's tea-party
we are treated to the crumbs from the tablecloth
of industrial-empire-death-by-numbers.

War is an onslaught of terrible mathematics.
Full-page diagrams in pastel shades formulate how many
former students sleep in a foreign field that *is* forever –

sculptors forge a new iron repose of the tourist age
to be mass-produced for the national mantelpiece
out of iron railings and working-class saucepans.

The Miners' Strike becomes a picnic with the police
on the village green, illustrated by time-lapse pictures
of coniferous coal lurking subterranean in a virgin seam.

Maps become useless.
Someone tows the whole collection of British Isles
further out into the Atlantic and cuts it adrift.

II *Geography*

Mud gurgle –
morning storming of thresholds
throwing up the silt of another harvest

and the coastal slip
of crumble-cliffs abrading
to the tumble of wooden matchsticks
into the Solent.

The rough semantics of tarmac
versus a thinning Antarctic shelf
is the thirst of a greater scheme.

All you have taught us
is the story
of our own
destructions.

III *Another Tongue*

A verb or noun
quite like this one.
The time, please.
A class of sharpening
anarchists plotting
a lunchtime coup
under the cover
of French grammar.

Manning barricades
for a word plucked
from the bible-paper-thin
passport pages
that open on
another world entirely
but refuse to navigate
on dialects.

Taste!
A verb in parallel
with my
barbed-wire kisses
and the words
ask me and I won't say no.
Ouvrez la fenêtre

IV *Sciences*

Nodding off in the polyester warmth
of an Army and Navy Store parka
and slowly awakening to the rainbow glow
of your own periodic table, the Bunsen burner's
sputtered-out blue beyond
and the door's open for walking.

Anything becomes possible;
the summer rain falls sideways,
the brave mock the laws of physics.
Wings melt. The sun breaks in
to mop the steamy brow of tarmac.
This is the nature of things
and don't let any teacher tell you different.

The Great Central's cut becomes a glimmering path,
scrumpy fruit overhung with briars and polythene –
the golden soulful answers you waited for – and,
skiving off, you find the footpath brings you
to high windows, the ripe red Victorian cloisters
of the boarding school's borders, disciplined wisteria
scaling summerhouses, chortling in the breeze.

An afternoon misspent in the study of gravity's trajectory;
stones chipping the verandahs of the elite.

v *Music*

In the monotone riot of another dead composer
we have chosen to write an anthem for the school.

It will be composed of skiving off and *suicide alley*,
the sound of civic pigeons colonising the silverware,

the clash of boy meets girl meets tragic ensemble of light
somewhere beyond the silos of a different town just like this.

It will be composed of all the kids left on the offside
when the time comes to pick the year's team of winners

and the distilled anger of the never-heard singer-songwriter's
broken gamut of strings, detuned to a finer chord of *O*.

Written on toilet walls, it will exist for three days,
four nights, before the janitorial chorus swash of bleach

makes better of the notes.

Sand

It began when you opened your desk
and found everything gone, replaced with sand.
You opened the wooden pencil case your brother
had made and it contained nothing but sand.
Next, your books filled with sand and the words
began to wear away. Your homework was late
because sand ate the sums and solutions.
Study time vanished in to the time it had taken
to dig the sand from the library shelves
like an archaeologist
before you could find the reference books.
When you were sent to fetch the register,
the secretary poured sand into your open hands.
At detention, you wrote out a hundred times
I must not lose the sand register on the way back to class.
When you opened the door to the classroom, a dune
of sand poured out that it was impossible to climb up.
The taps in the toilets only gave you sand, cold pale sand.
Your running shoes were emptied of sand, but still
the sand got between your toes and blistered your feet.
Sand followed you home, waited at the bus stop,
filled the back seat of the coach and slid down the aisle
when the driver braked harshly.
Sand lurked throughout weekends, bank holidays,
every day of the half-term break. Sand accumulated
on Sunday evenings and came down on you
in a storm after tea, filled your sheets with a million
tiny silica jibes, made it impossible to sleep
and got into your dreams, even there;
when the other children laughed,
the sand blasted your face, clogged your throat.

On the New Bypass

We are all wondering if the girl in the tree will stop crying;
she's three boughs up and missing one trainer,
her weeping a persistent radio jingle above the traffic.

On the bypass, by the traffic lights, two women take turns
to photograph each other, a mother/daughter pairing
who have fallen into existence through a fashion-shoot.

A student with easel and canvas astride the central reservation
takes down the cement factory's likeness, but nothing rectifies
the architect's evil eye and the flat grey flanks of his nightmare.

Things seem put wrongly, out of key as a cover version
mockery of how it once was or should be; slurred video
on low-bandwidth, lips dancing out of sync with the words.

We seem to be moving along without gaining ground,
giving way to actors who do a better job of the poor drama,
shifting to the sidings of our own roadside attractions.

The vanishing point of the bypass bisects and turns on itself.
I'm not sure now if we travel towards light or away from it,
or if the girl in the tree will stop crying, if she'll ever come down.

Fabrikgeist

Sometimes referred to affectionately as *Old-Jack-of-Trades*.
Has familiars, often taking the form of machinery animated
without explanation, or a singular, lonesome whistling.

The shop floor is purgatory. The spirit can only be exorcised
by the removal of blueprints, the emptying of lockers
and the smelting of several thousand taps, dies and drills.

This spirit has a mischievous sense of humour
which has been broken by three decades of rain, rust,
and under-investment, and is prone to haunting sites

of last employment. It cannot be bottled by priest, policeman
or doctor. Its presence is signified by greasy overalls, missing tea cups,
footprints from a pair of safety boots, leading nowhere.

The Shop-floor Gospel

Angry –
he who trudges the grey
dog-eared estate avenues,
a rasp of
I bloody told you so
ready on their lips.

Fortune-teller, free agent,
laughter in grubby canteens;
Mark my words.
We're a living museum!
There's no future.
We're sold, sold out –

Decades blowing a coarse wind
through the resistance,
where no borders were left
to cross, no other line to join,
only the holding out against
believing in some kind of *new*
that pacified the absences
with retail parks.

You are
the lone *no*
on the shop-floor –
the habitual reader
of all the wrong news,
the public library ghost,
the vote cast for some
Old School
that's long since closed.

A vanished oddment
a piss in the wind
the autumn leaves
laughing
at a glib historian's
reworking
of the lady's
not for turning.
I bloody told you so.

Coventry is

You know, Wordsworth said of Coventry that was one of the
most beautiful cities in all of England. It is a pity...a great pity

One Night in November (Belgrade Theatre, Coventry)

always the bridesmaid and never the bride,
    is somewhere to be sent,

where you come to find your train of thoughts
    and miss the last train home,

where things come to end and the opening paragraph
    is rewritten, then lost, then bodged,

where hope is exchanged for something a little less brash,
    like *maybe, perhaps*,

an ugly/beautiful place that seeks someone
    to love it back,

misses the letters you used to write home
    and wishes you would call,

preferring not to talk, tonight, of the masses buried
    at London Road, the dead car plants, assembly lines,

rarely loved, much maligned, occasionally
    extra-marital, a clandestine affair,

too old and worn out for *that* kind of
    funny business,

disgusted, outraged at the suggestion and only needs
    a good architect to get rid of the dark roots,

wants you to know that she didn't always
    look this way,

going to raise a little soul and get herself
    back on that bloody horse.

Midlands kids,

we were raised in cars, grew up on the back seats
of the long-gone marques of British manufacturing,
Morris, Austins and Talbots, slightly crap even new,
third- or fourth-hand, pockmarked, and in summer
distinguished by the waft of hot leatherette, the oil-black
tang of four-star fumes and the rust-red frothing of a had-it
head-gasket that had sent the radiator broiling over.

Those people we once thought to be, then – misplaced
down the gap in the back seat that so ingeniously folded forward,
or left tucked like secrets in the chrome pop-out passengers' ashtrays;
just as each promised holiday and magical mystery tour silvered
in the wing-mirrors momentarily before vanishing far out
on the hot horizon, like the car plants, company overalls, jobs for life,
the legendary square steering wheel of a paintshop-fresh Allegro.

Our Old Lady of the Rain

She was older, iron-tasting tang,
the smell of damp girders about her.
She'd had blueprints once, hundreds of them,
kept in a plan chest, maplewood drawers
as wide as a kitchen table, and as deep.

Knew where to fall from one day to the next,
kept her chancels swept clean and free of ghosts
but filled roofless factories with rust and the lathes
coked up with the ruddy mould. She couldn't help it,
and was sad to be a Midas inside-out.

I loved her, though I didn't know if I should.

Love Song for the Ordnance Survey

What measure of time is sluicing
through the dappling rings of immortal hills?

What weight the hollow-hearted burial mounds,
Saxon naves, felled steeples, tribal hill-forts,
ventilation mine-shafts, brick-born water towers,
analogue Cold War transmitters, pillbox viewpoints?

What radius the boundary arcs,
the stamina of forests' greened retreat
beaten back at the speckled blots of settlement,
the shaded/sloped river ruts, the symmetry of hangars?

What current the canals, descending the lock's silent-shift,
coal boats and Staffordshire china rising in the hulls
and sidelined, quickened by the railways
rising beside motorways, rising onwards?

What depth the medicinal baths, restoring spas
sought by new townsfolk, the tumulus of mill races
gone save for great unworking gears turning nothing
in damp summering fields?

And what volume the settlements,
slumbering in bracketed old-world italics,
inherited after-other names, lost or erased,
the monikers of places declassified?

What velocity the shifting coastlines
vanishing faster than any paper can skip a heartbeat to?
(and the winter peaks absolved in mists that can neither
be seen or heard, let alone measured?)

Of all the demarcations multiplied
kept in their latitudinal squares, of each known
and unknown quantity, let us sing
of detail and capacity, the map's measured love.

Border Dispute

I don't break a mirror, pick the clear thorns
from the sink, this time I don't take the car keys,

and the neighbours won't hear us, because this
time I tear up and rejoin the maps instead,

and am redrafting the territories again, tonight.
You ask if we should make these boroughs ours,

streets that detail the marbled thighs of hillsides,
that are spilling out as the map lets them go

like stuffing from a bad pillow, bought too cheaply.
The A-roads too are being lost beneath an argument

of latitudinal lines, and again the parish of black and red,
the lines of the danger zone, the firing range:

this is my fear. Gather them up, sweetheart,
put the Great Central back and redraw our borders.

This new map says what happened, tells why.
The land west of here doesn't apologise.

On Discovery
(for William Smith and his 1815 Geological Map)

I

What is any place built upon
but accumulated silt and memory?
National bandwidth of clay, shale, coal
and lime, industrial curse-blessing.
Where the old roads build on above,
the coming revolution blasts
a new path deep into the bedrock.

II

The earth's own book of revelations:
the stone flora of ancient sea shallows
awakening dormant topographic tides
in cutting and quarry. Opening a vein
to spill the riches of the long dead;
echinoid palm-stone, ammonite spiral scratch,
crinoid sea-lily branching to a bloom
at the very second of demise.

III

Above all, the high-tea strata upon English lawns;
a layer-cake of manners, snobbery and new ideas.
The naming, schooling, placing of who's who,
the posting assigned you must not rise above.
The trick is push on regardless, anticline,
a troublesome kink in the rock structure.

IV

Of those who plagiarise, mock-mavens,
graft-thieves, who heft your ideas as their own,
re-draw your maps, re-colour and ink the loam
with borrowed genius, profit from your leaps
of faith but tip no hat to you, William:
know that not one of their names matters now,
the stones and maps know properly of yours;
the debt and the loan, the outstanding credit.

V

Back to the earth, below a ring of eight bells
at St Peter's, a church stood first in wood, then in stone,
and later stone again, iron- and limestone
weathering Northamptonshire sun and rain.
The question of perspective remains; under pressure,
how knowledge like sediment accumulates –
in daring and taking of a new vantage, a cut-through
the ground on which we stand and stand on still,
you drew in rugged spectrum the whole isles anew.

Odds On

Where do the racehorses sleep?
Red Rum, Dawn Run and Arkle
sleep now, the broken neck,
Aintree grave, front-page obit.

Himself, Ireland, no longer
a twice-a-day Guinness drinker
but a museum curio, steeplechaser
skeleton strung out in a glass stable.

Time and form. The Liffey awash
with good tidings, tigers sighted
out near Connemara. A Japanese
4x4 and a racehorse in every drive.

Going good to firm. New estates
finicking up on the hills in a rash
of prosperity. The money men
talk a good sport, their pockets empty.

Who pays when the rains come?
The going's none so good,
the economy shot and bolted,
the abattoir the only game in town.

Where do the racehorses sleep?
Red Rum, Dawn Run and Arkle
long gone under the sod. Mass graves
for the trophy ponies. Sleep now.

Seven Horse Secrets

The horse's heart is a grand mansion of four piston-firing chambers.

A horse sees a world blurred in the two-tone flourish of the photo finish.

Look into the amber planet of a horse's eye and a refracted universe forms there.

Horses turn the turf of an ever-moving, never-quite-touched earth beneath their hooves.

Horses laugh at our expense; lips peeled, ivory-gravestone teeth bared, domino pieces unplaced.

Horses are melancholic humourists; they know of the pending darkness beyond the five-bar gate, beyond the green paddock. Hancock learned all he knew from horses.

Horses tramp the ancient treadmill of our whims, trot to our bidding, broken, bought and sold, but only ever possess themselves.

Dog, on First Being Named

They're wrong, of course, our owners who think
they own us; choice an illusion, out of their hands
quicker than a quicksilver whippet out the traps.

But the name at least, this two-syllable moniker,
and the telephone manner with which you deliver it,
is yours to give, a password for recall, bringing me to heel

and to your hand's peace offering, rubber-nosing your scent
to sniff out invisible trails of all your laughter and grievings,
of daffodils and thunder, the rec's muddy turf, thawing snow.

From this first, it's your voice that cracks instinct, unlocks
obedience, echoes through each leg-twitching dream, pursued
across each field; you naming our bond, my wordless joy.

Later, you teach me code words for how I must ask, lie, play
dead. But it's my name I'll chase down, hounding to your cry,
in the long over-arm pitch of all the dog days to come.

The hearts of everyone in this room

are curled as little fists flexing under ribs,
moving the blood's freight beneath skin,
between bridge spans of bone and muscle,
filling each with their own fierce song.

Each, beginning with another's jump start,
takes the swing and fall of days to come
as a boxer's skipping rope whistling through air,
our simple, agnostic, metronome's prayer.

Companion, flaw-father, our own invigilator,
flooding the body with a full spectrum's light,
tuning the radar of its echolocation to quicken
in the presence of another's quickening beat;

proof then, even in our age of surfaces, that
what is hidden, messy, within, still matters.

Script Notes from the lost episode of *The Future*

Satellite images from the depths of space
mark out an ex-industrial tundra;
the shammy camouflage of enterprise zones,
the vortex of estates and vast retail shacks
hitched-up on borrowed cash; the foot of
the burial chamber, not the font of a powerhouse.

Zoom in on the seized engines of heartsick towns,
haemorrhaging hoardings and economy food,
knackered out with plastic knick-knackery and poverty,
and trace the familiar terrain of utter defeat:
who won here isn't as obvious as who was beaten
in battles fought and lost generations back.

Sharp focus on heartlands become poundlands, groinlands,
lost beyond the brash new suburbs pickpocketing each other,
and unrecognisable to a visitor returning, light-years on,
following a storyline of broken pickets, museum banners,
hope fossilised, dry lips incanting truths with no home,
a long, slow whistle echoing into the dark matter of dead streets.

Cut now to sepia crowds gathered outside lit halls, ornate doors locked,
double-barrelled and double-bolted; cut to starched collar and cuff.
Rolling news-feed bleats a mockery of the voiceless, *Hark at you!*
Noses up to the bright windows of aspirational ownership,
warm within the deep velvet radiance of obvious wealth.
Without, hungry winter blows a coarse invective over its teeth.

UnWeather

unweder: 'storm' in Old English, meaning literally 'un-weather'

I

There will be nights like this
when, under the dark sky's heavy knife,
the dog comes to your heel and you both stare
far off into the fathomless middle-distance of 3 a.m.
And there will be mornings like this too,
when dread moves in you like botulism
as the little island tilts on its foundations,
threatens to tip you and the seasick dog loose,
alone together on the burning edge as longshore drift
carries the crumbling biscuit nation off to sea
and you will have nothing left but the words
of an old song on your lips, the bones of a last meal
to pick through, the ashes, ashes everywhere.

II

We need a new word for the name of the country
that I woke up in this morning
We need a new word for the theft
of something indefinable but definitely lifted
We need a new word with which to curse
the salesmen of a shoddy nightmare
We need a new word for the sense of betrayal
that smashes the pedestals of household gods
We need a new word for how we navigate conversations
feeling our way in to work out where the fractures lie
We need a new word for a nation that doesn't exist
We need a new word for how the bigotry in the mortar
became the bricks and stones and broken windows

We need a new word for walking the grey streets
of each new day with a mouth full of lime and ashes
We need a new word for the uncertainty of loss
We need a new word for regret
We need a new word for the new bad news
We need a new word for the ugliness of our new words
For shame, we need a new word for the shame
We need a new word for the fear

III

Our tongues were made from
Sprechen, dicere, parler,
mackled together with flints and flaps
of leather, wolf pelt, sheepskins,
grown greenly fat in the sun, pressed,
stoppered in amphora and bartered,
molten to lead in the crucible and poured
into typeface punches, licked onto vellum,
all carried in language's little sailboat,
my tongue might have said *labhairt*
where it now says *speak*,
each leaf of English borrowed from
a starry European library of tongues,
library card now revoked, and the tongues,
rabbling and clattering through vowels and dialect
and regional collateral like wonderful
mongrels escaped from the pound,
never to be returned, gifts
we must carry behind our teeth,
a *Hleów-feðer* to drape on
a fellow traveller's shoulders.

Hleów-feðer means 'shelter-feather', but in some Old English literature it is
used mean to put a protecting arm put around someone.

IV

I want to take what my neighbour has.
I want the car he has on his drive, which is newer than the car on my drive,
I want to take the crockery and the food and the cool beer from his table,
I want to take his workaday whistling on a frosty morning,
I want to take the quiet pride of his smiling family, his carefree son
kicking the football, switching lightly from left to right foot
with same ease he slips between one language and another.

    I want to piss a stream of Rule Britannia over their flowerbeds,
    I want to wave my flag and tell them they're not welcome,
    grind our differences into their faces, pack their bags, *Send 'em back.*
I want a sepia empire with a post-truth currency,
I want to scrub the star from the union,
take down the blue from their sky.

V

I lost my country
for the promises on a big red bus
I lost my country
when someone left the handbrake off
and it rolled away downhill
I lost my country
after it was recalled due to
a manufacturing fault
and then burst into flames
I lost my country
to stop someone else enjoying it
I lost my country
to the failure of the left
to an offshore account
I lost my country
in the food bank queue
on the playing fields of Eton

Reasoning

It wasn't as imagined. Not hand drawn,
or a home movie in stuttering 8mm,

But suddenly diffusing, a salt-solution in
an acid bath brimming with gold.

Nor was it meant to unfold like this,
to come unpinned and unmounted

as the movement of two shadows as they bind
and separate through different species of dark.

The speck of a star in your eyes, the grit
working loose from the oyster.

Three Sketches for Dreams

Dream One

A wren has got into the house
through a window carelessly left open.

A butterfly net cannot catch, nor a saucepan,
nor a tea-towel. It is framing a complex song,

a three-note peeping that teases and ranges
and pities your attempts at setting it free.

If only the wren, this bundle of bone and tune,
would be freed, it could paint a song once again

in the places where it should hang, between the willow's
dappling branches, in the arc of the garden's shade.

I'll paint it here instead, whilst I can. Damn you,
And damn your plans for me. This song

is for rooms you have failed to fill
with another music.

Dream Two

is a child lost, publicly,
perhaps in a woodland heart crowded

with the disembodied voices of evening walkers
between mossy trees and barbed-wire briars,

where a folktale should be set out with a woodcutter,
his wife and some gloomy force built of straw and mud.

Your feet and heart thudding, leaf mulch
underfoot, or on the gummy pavements

of a busy high street, a blur of plastic signage
and street furniture, gormless strangers

who look back blankly when you ask
if they have seen a child that you can't describe,

leaving bare, bloody footprints everywhere you run.

Dream Three

The neighbours have come to remove your garden.
They do not agree with your free-ranging attitude

of wild jasmine twinning pendants high above fence panels,
the honeysuckle plunging old wood hard and pungent

through the places where the wall has crumbled.
An old clambering pinkish rose should not flower

this late into autumn, so each bud has been precisely
secateured to within an inch of three year's growth.

They have cleared the dead deep-reddish hydrangea heads
and sterilised the fractious *Clematis Montana*, wild

with pale bell-stars, to a pruned stalk, a cruciform of bye-laws,
all broken rules and borders you have crossed.

Double Exposure

Where's that other woman now?
That plastercast saint, *martyr for all old Ireland.*

I caught sight of her last going for the deep end,
moving fast though the waters of that new life.

Now she's trapped in the white light of the flash,
overexposed, on the bench in the municipal park.

She says nothing. Such statues speak so little,
but her lips edge open as if there is something to say,

about the night she walked, why she went her way,
why she sits now under the willow's wide brimming green.

Old wood will shoot new for spring.
It is only me who waves to you, alone, from the window.

Gasbagging

Excuse the carrion sisters their roadkill,
there has been so little gossip
that now it's my bones they pick over.

Too slim about the neck, too wide of ankle,
never says as much as a mystery,
hasn't given a moment's thought...

Nothing vegetable, mineral or animal,
nothing stirring between those thighs (*too wide*)
but desire's secret, damp and selfish nights.

Be grateful for your half-good looks, your girlish gifts
or scrub the red-tiled doorsteps of eternity:
this is their word.

Folklore

First, it was the children who danced out in the radiant twilight,
the black dust; there was nothing else pretty to tell in their tale.

Next, came the monsters made out of men and women
who took to their beds and rotted to a burnt-out hull.

Then the rumour of the invisible fire that seared and scalded
any who fought it, the rivers and forests too overrun

by something alive beyond guns or even God. No one
came back to talk of it, and such stories, disputed by the radio

and all the wisdom of official statements – plain folklore –
until the photographs, the reports, the fire-fighters

who had walked into the meltdown in rubber boots
finally spoke for them all.

Shrug

Nothing happened for years:
the concept of opposition
clearly outmoded and uncouth.
Automated text proclaimed:
> *Become a limb in our service economy!*
> *Opportunities for electronic serfdom in all sectors*
> *of our growing waste-paper empire.*

Reports revealed how *plucky strivers*
sort soiled rags for the workfare team.
The shrug became our national salute;

in small scandals of stolen, littered lives
or *en masse*, the poorest slandered,
the doorsteps of the status quo swept clean
we slumped at the headlines and hoopla and shrugged.
Gone viral, even our selfies betrayed us,
looking inward at ourselves infinite,
at our own *what-to-be-done*, unable
to bite the hand that fed us
our daily national dish of lies,
such cold, damnable lies.

How we fell in love with big data

The data spoke and we knelt
    to hear its message.
The data drummed its fingers so we posted
    pictures of bijou cupcake happiness.

The pie chart distribution tells us
    which sector has disposable wealth.
(You can quietly dispose of
    those other sectors.)

Tell us who you are, the market value
    of your catchment-area house
in a rising suburb, the profit potential
    of the one you wake up next to,

the size of your income expectations, pre-tax,
    the passwords printed on your leather slip-on soles;
the trailing footprint traces you leave behind
    when you think no one else is looking.

A Skyped voice reminds us that social media data
    is ripe for the picking, a fat summer gold field,
we the obedient ears of wheat
    awaiting the harvest blade.

How the Town Lost Its Song

I

What is to be sung now, if a hymn
is to find the voice of this forgettable town?
The colour's bled out and even maps

have little to say for themselves but this;
how now the new plateau territories
are only mazes or mouse traps,

postcoded realms, private terrains.
When sun lifts the raw morning, gather the scrim
of demolition, broken bricks, concrete, dust.

What's lost is just that, and there's
no point recasting it now, or wondering
how renegade harmonies once sought a home

as one hand to another, finding its way to words;
how it came that the refrain was sold out
and sung now only of what can be bought.

II

First, sell the ground beneath,
places where our feet touch the familiar,

If there are connections, sever and invert them,
fence and cleanse. Surface-dress, dredge topsoil.

Enclosure is a sudden art.
No one should understand the artist's intentions.

Make the song's movement impossible in the old modes,
erase tracks, and by tracks, memory, lines.

Wipe the ferric tapes clean
of all recordings that might incriminate.

Make *private* and *trespass*
clear doctrines; monetise the hinterlands.

III

What is to be sung now,
        forgotten town?

Tell me what it felt like
        when you finally came down,

space cadets fast-forwarded,
        finding themselves earthed junkies.

While you were away,
        men in hi-vis yellow took down

the miraculous sunset
        over the turbine works

and whitewashed out the space-age
        squall of monitor feedback,

told us all, in the local paper,
        to dream small and think a lot less;

hoping for better only makes
        hometown life restive, alcohol-tinged.

We miss your visions, but the shelves
        of the pharmacy/armoury are empty.

Forgettable town,
        the final analogue coda has long faded out

from the speakers.
        We live our lives in mono.

The poem written to settle an old score is

a bent penny jamming the mind's jukebox,
a long-distance non-contact bloodsport,
a biscuit tin of fireworks under the stairs of a matchstick house,
a maladjusted guard dog who bites his handler in misguided affection,
a rodent's corpse floating, as yet undetected, in a drinking-water tank,
something future generations will not thank you for.

Lonely Hearts

By
the time you
realise, it's too late.
My entire spectrum
of towering, infra-red rage
will blow the filaments of all the bulbs
on the parade of pretty memories.
Being not much to look at is my first footprint
on the unmade bed of your heart;
unassuming, with my shark's under-bite,
I scent the blood of single parent, recent divorce,
fathoms off, the milky desperation for an adult conversation,
maybe more. I draw a vision for you of how it will be;
the rooms of your home we'll fill with me,
the way I'll keep you strung on
my words like rosary beads.
I'll squat in your lives,
a tinder box
waiting for
a stray
spark.

Landmarks

Our geographies are different,
pierced by landmarks like this:
secluded lanes, alleyways, parks,
emptying train carriages, taxi cabs,
stairwells, public toilets, almost all
open spaces when unaccompanied.

Or those other landscapes of threat:
working late alone, short-cuts home,
the party where the first drink swipes
your running feet from under you,
the stranger or the friend you trusted.

It can happen almost anywhere.
And too often, it does.
We roll up this tattooed map,
carry it everywhere we go.

Disturbed,

a blackbird's nest of bug-eyed chicks,
gummy pink, inked with the tattoos of feathers
yet to fledge, will be abandoned, and the adult
pair won't come back to them even after
you retreat to the patio and keep watch,

the dusk air full of the alarm calls telling on
your deed, the battery running out, silence
growing in the cupped bowl of twig and leaf.
Gone too far, you've revealed all that is held
within the fragile heart of things;

how easily they are to be broken,
how impossible to repair.

Dresden Papers

(after Matthew Picton's 'Dresden, 1945')

1 *Guidebook*

Gemstone on the Elba; a polished baroque pearl, how the river
bends an embracing elbow through this most elegant of cities.
Best visited in the springtime, but now sudden and unseasonal.
The honeycomb colony of streets, palaces and pleasure gardens
now thread with whispers, refugees from the east. Observe this;
how an ill-rumouring wind disturbs the birds gathering on the
ivory dome of the Frauenkirche and across the evening's emptying
squares. The guide-map blooms, tar-charred and gap-toothed.

2 *Diary*

The page turns between February 13th
and Ash Wednesday, black-edged.
firestorm reduces all other paperwork
to flakes; not snow, yet the sky lit
with belated Christmas lights.
Paper-thin walls fall like dominoes;
the entombed amassed from cellar to cellar.
Fahrenheit breaks the confines of glass.
The pen that would detail the next entry
seared dry of ink, does not write again.

3 *Libretto*

Flamethrowers hiss the shocked verse on the impromptu plaza
of a flattened city. Here was once. Now, a dazed civilian chorus,
inheriting only ashes and charcoal's rancorous caesura.

fire scorches the score from the stave, sound from tongue and throat.
Go and speak nothing of this. Maps alone recall in requiem;
fading contour lines, awkward silences and troubled leitmotifs.

Only slow decades will reform the city's whorled thumbprint;
give back the words with which the street's aria is sung.

The Ghost Light

Burning centre-stage in an empty house,
a single light-bulb, its filament

bursting the white hot sun of a bright idea
in its small glass brain. Without it,

hazards loom and multiply in the unlit theatre,
the main switch stage-left means on entrance

you slowly touch-feel your way, counting through
the stalls on the velvet nap of upflipped seat rows

and, as your eyes adjust in the dusty dark,
sight the great prow of the stage forming,

vast and empty in the gloom, feeling along the edge
its statuesque hull for the steps up, stage left,

avoiding the yawning orchestra pit and stepping
into the tarry dark behind the curtain

where scenery and ropes and hoists and all manner
of hazard lay coiled and baited, wild luck itself,

hands faltering over flaking plaster for the master switch
that will awake the playhouse's great slumbering hearth,

lighting you safely, all the way back across the house, out
to the box office and the stained and gum-spattered carpet

setting only goodness and wonder and a thousand dozy motes
in the house lights at your back and lighting all your way.

Otters, Avon

Two magic tricks conjured
from a town river's unlikely shallows;
brown and paintbrush-slick,

their periscope heads above
almost-still water, lithe suggestion
of swimming bodies below.

Two question marks,
quizzical, near-vanishing under
the ebb until reappearing

downstream between green rushes,
aces pulled from a sleeve,
sleight of the early year's light;

dusk holding its breath,
they dip and vanish for good
into the river's hem.

Shrapnel

Collect the secrets: nuclear trains thrumming
through the gantried station in blackout hours,
Soviet missiles rumoured for the radio station
in an ever-November of seventies hostility
and the cement works puffing mushroom patinas
out over the town, settling
    sinister summer snow –

learning such things about this town
could keep you wide-eyed
from the dowdy two-tone of sleep.
Such things could turn you over in dreams,
key rattling in rusty lock,
    ignition stalling for a hotwire.

Echoes in the terraces,
dog-legging streets that spur out across
the valley-slope, and out there, somewhere,
the Dobunni and Coritanni re-enacting,
one to the other, over a woodlands swathe
    from hill fort to hill fort through lamp-lit trees.

Such things could keep the light-sleepers
twitching the town's curtains, waiting for
a dawn, a creaking morning to come at last
with the milk float's retrospective whirr.
Such things, cataclysms, strange new worlds
    coming sudden to uproot the civic chrysants,

    tampering the foundations of the jubilee clock,
rendering a map of a shadow town, toxic moss
growing thick across municipal lawns –

such sudden things might never come.
Yet, waking each morning to a town
      which has reassembled its skyline, reordered

      the scenery, left a gap where the tall-storeyed
chapels of turbine test-houses once caught the gold
simmering dusk in galleries of windows,
it is no such little thing to vanish. The town sleeps
      and wakes, reshapes another day –

         what name to give to such small change?

Dobunni and *Coritanni*: Iron Age tribes with a presence in Warwickshire in pre-Roman times.

Around the Rectory

A strange suggestion in the evening air;
early May, just on the brink of sun,
waving another era goodbye as it hops a taxi,
to go to ground, for a spin *around the rectory*,
to lick wounds, let history file copy,
hoping for it to be kinder than reality.

It doesn't look back at us, waving and a touch
drunk on the melancholia of nostalgia.
Bad-mannered, greedy guest, we knew you
all too well. The flaws, the appalling things
you'd done (could it have been much worse?)
Now they're packing you a suitcase,
stacking your books in the hall, drawing lots
for the mohair coat. You start to wonder
where it all went wrong,

the honeymoon before betrayal and bad omen,
or after the back-slapping and the bubbly-on-the-house.
Between the taxi's diesel chug and the news reader's
low static, between old friends and clean sheets
remains the drone of a disembodied voice,
that wanted *history to be my judge* but hadn't soap
enough to wash the bloody handshake clean.

Circa

Night as rag-soaked petroleum,
the whisper of moon creaks
through the cloud's machinery.

Something has taken a hold
that leaves you wondering
where it all began –

with milk turning thick-sour
clotted in the bottle, or the soft
gyrations of motorway noise

trapped in lobes of the landscape's
shell-coils, a spark caught
silently as a kiss threatens a dithering island.

Homing

It is slow and calcifying as Midlands tap water –
you don't notice it until one day you realise
you don't belong in these manicured places;

belonging a wilder chorus that cannot
be found here, in between a choice
of demitasse spoons or matching stationery,

sugared whispers where the fault lines of class
are never far from the surface of conversation,
though it will ache to know this.

Odd then, this squareness of feeling,
this round wholeness of being apart, homesick
for a place where there are no manners to feign.

Go, and trust the streets to carry you solo to where
the terraces loop with love's familiar brogue, where
a lone bird sings to catch the reel of itself echoing.

Poem in which a small dog looks into the sun

and half closes her amber eyes as if everything's replete
on this back doorstep, small garden, nondescript town,
where the washing waves our shadows from the line.

The year is faltering on the slack rope of seasons;
clematis and jasmine twine the breeze flowerless,
sound carrying the rumble roar of mainline and freight

high above us, September's last blue vaulted ceiling
and we together worship outdoors beneath it,
this small domestic god and I, for the warmth on our bones

for needing nothing more than this sun, this garden.
There is so much that could be said about
the commonplace miracle of being here in this moment.

THANKS

Thank you to those whose encouragement over the years has made this book possible and who have helped my poetry-writing in a multitude of ways: Jill Abram, Jo Bell, Liz Berry, Peter Blegvad, Zoë Brigley-Thompson, Robbie Burton, Peter Carpenter, Jonathan Davidson, Roz Goddard, Robert Harper, David Hart, Michael Hulse, Gregory Leadbetter, Michael McKimm, David Morley, Peter Raynard, Jacqui Rowe, Jonathan and Maria Taylor, and George Ttoouli. And of course, especial thanks are due, with much love, to Kevin and Cindy.

Thank you to Neil Astley and to Bloodaxe for their belief in my poems and for making *Assembly Lines* a reality.

Thanks are due also to the Warwick Writing Programme at the University of Warwick and Writing West Midlands' Room 204 Writer Development Programme for supporting the writing of these poems at various stages, and to the Jerwood Compton Poetry Fellowship for their generosity and support.

All my love and much gratitude as always to Mum & Dad and Mark, for nurturing my love of words from the very start, and for all of your support along the way.